# A Walk in Chittaranjan Park

Siva Prasad Bose and Joy Bose

Published by Joy Bose, 2022.

# A Walk in Chittaranjan Park

## Little Kolkata in New Delhi

By Siva Prasad Bose and Joy Bose

Published by Joy Bose

# Contents

# Dedication

This book is dedicated to all the past, present and future residents of Chittaranjan Park.

# Preface

Chittaranjan Park or CR park is a residential colony in South Delhi, bordered by Greater Kailash 1 and 2 and located close to areas such as Nehru place, Alaknanda, Kalkaji and Govindpuri. It is sometimes called "Little Kolkata" because of the Kolkata style street food, Bengali culture and festivals celebrated here.

Previously called EPDP Colony or East Pakistan Displaced Persons Colony and Purbachal, CR Park is a Bengali dominated colony that was originally developed to house refugees of partition from East Bengal, but has recently become more diverse. It is a cultural treat famous for its celebration of Durga Puja, Bengali snacks and sweets.

In this book we discuss the famous landmarks and festivals in CR Park. This is intended to be partly a travel guide for those who want to experience this microcosm of Bengali culture in New Delhi.

Our own Bose family has been resident in Delhi for a very long time, originally residing in Kashmere Gate and later moving to CR Park.

# About the authors

Siva Prasad Bose is a writer of introductory guides on aspects of law in India and a retired electrical engineer. He received his electrical engineering degree from Jadavpur University, Kolkata and has a law degree from Meerut University, Meerut.

Siva has been a resident of CR Park in New Delhi for more than 15 years. He previously lived with his family at Kashmere Gate in Old Delhi, attended Bengali Boys' School in Kashmere Gate and was an active participant and football player in the Bengali club, also in Kashmere Gate.

Joy Bose is a researcher and data scientist with an LLM from Golden Gate University, San Francisco.

# Chapter 1: History of Chittaranjan Park and Bengalis in Delhi

In this chapter we discuss briefly about the history of Bengalis in Delhi and of CR Park.

## 1.1 British and Pre-British Era

Bengalis in Delhi have existed since the Mughal times. However, their population received a boost when the capital of India was shifted by the British from Kolkata to Delhi in 1911 and many Bengali government servants from Kolkata migrated to Delhi.

Most of the Bengalis settled in areas of old Delhi in the 20th century such as Kashmere Gate, Tis Hazari, Gol Market, Minto Road and also RK Puram. The oldest of the Kali mandirs and Durga Pujas in Delhi are around the same locations.

Cultural institutions like the Bengali club in Kashmere Gate and schools like the Bengali School were formed in early 20th century.

Figure: Building of the Bengali senior Secondary School in Kashmere Gate, also site of the Kashmere Gate Durga Puja

Figure: Entrance to Minto Road Durga Puja, one of the earliest continuous Durga Pujas in Delhi

Figure: Priest performing the arati of Goddess Durga at Kashmere gate Durga puja, a puja with history of more than 100 years

Figure: Entrance to New Delhi Kali Bari in Gole Market

## 1.2 Immigration of Bengalis After Partition

The next big wave of Bengali immigration to Delhi came in the 1940s and 1950s, when the partition brought many Hindu Bengalis from East Bengal or East Pakistan (later Bangladesh after 1972). Many of the new Bengalis immigrants originally settled in Kashmere Gate and other areas where Bengalis were residing, as well as some of the refugee colonies for refugees from Punjab.

The East Bengal Displaced Persons (EBDP) Association was formed in 1954 to support and take care of the displaced persons of the partition from East Bengal.

Many of the formerly displaced persons from Bengal who moved to Delhi and were mostly from the middle class, soon started working in various government or private jobs in Delhi as per their qualifications.

After a sustained period of petitions, the Indian government in early 1960s allocated a piece of land to the Bengalis in what was originally a forested and rocky area. The original allotees were given plots of land upon showing some proof of their property in East Bengal. More than 2000 plots were allotted in this way. After that, many of the new refugees moved to that location. Many started to construct their houses on the allotted plots and moved in soon after.

For reference, a similar plot of land was also given by the Indian government to Hindu Punjabis who came from West Punjab to Delhi after the partition and was named Lajpat Nagar after the freedom fighter Lala Lajpat Rai.

The Bengali colony was originally called EPDP colony (East Pakistan Displaced Persons Colony) and Purbachal and later renamed as Chittaranjan Park (CR Park for short) after the respected freedom fighter Deshbandhu Chittaranjan Das.

The Delhi Development Authority or DDA also helped in constructing many of the original houses in CR Park, as well as building a separate residential colony in nearby Kalkaji.

## 1.3 Development of CR Park Colony

Soon the forested and rocky areas of CR Park developed into a residential colony, complete with a Shiva temple and Kali temple on top of the hill, cultural institutions such as Bangiya Samaj and Chittaranjan memorial society, a Bengali medium school and markets where one could buy Bengali food, newspapers from Kolkata, and other supplies. Bengali festivals such as Durga Puja and Poush Mela began to be celebrated as well. Much of the development happened in the 1970s and 1980s.

Nowadays CR Park is considered an affluent and upscale colony in South Delhi. Due to rise in house prices generally and especially in South Delhi, getting a flat here for rent or buying is relatively expensive.

As an example, monthly rents for a 2BHK flat in CR Park typically range from Rs. 30,000 to over Rs. 70,000 as of 2025–26, depending on size and floor. Flats for sale are priced upwards of Rs. 2.5–4 crore, with builder floors averaging around Rs. 23,000–27,000 per sq ft. Property values have risen by over 40% in the last five years, reflecting CR Park's continued desirability as one of South Delhi's most sought-after addresses.

References:

- https://www.99acres.com/property-for-rent-in-cr-park-south-delhi-ffid
- https://www.99acres.com/property-rates-and-price-trends-in-cr-park-south-delhi-prffid

CR Park is divided into blocks of houses. The original layout comprised eleven blocks from A to K. In the 1990s, an additional 714 displaced families were accommodated, resulting in further blocks designated M, N, O, P, K-1, K-2, as well as the pockets known as Pocket 40 (Navapalli) and Pocket 52 (Dakhinpalli). Each of these blocks has one or more parks that are used as children's playgrounds, as a space for morning or evening walks and yoga exercises and also for erecting pandals to celebrate Durga Puja and other festivals.

The older-style houses that were originally constructed in the 1970s and 1980s by the original allotees of the plots, have typically one to three floors, but many of the modern multi-flat houses constructed by builders may have 4 or even more floors. Therefore, there is an interesting mix of architecture. The older style houses have typically bigger rooms with higher roofs and are fewer storied with no lifts. Often, when a patriarch in a joint family dies, their children may choose to get a builder to remodel the house with more stories.

There are now a number of retired people living in the area, since the original allotees of the flats have mostly retired or are quite old.

One of the most cherished social traditions that CR Park has preserved is the Bengali custom of "adda" — the leisurely, informal gathering of friends and neighbours for animated conversation, storytelling, and debate. In the evenings, the market corners, tea stalls and park benches of CR Park come alive with this uniquely Bengali pastime that cuts across age and background. This tradition of adda is considered a hallmark of Bengali bhadralok (genteel) culture, and CR Park remains one of the few places in Delhi where it still flourishes naturally.

Figure: Recently constructed multi-floor flat complexes in CR Park

Figure: Some of the older style multi-storied houses

## 1.4 Conclusion

The journey of Bengalis to Delhi, from the Mughal era to the waves of post-partition migration, has shaped not only their lives but also the character of neighborhoods like CR Park. Understanding this layered history helps us appreciate how the colony developed into a thriving Bengali hub. In the next chapter, we will explore the physical manifestation of this evolution by walking through the important buildings and landmarks that define CR Park today.

# Chapter 2: Important Buildings and Landmarks

---

Despite being a relatively recent colony in New Delhi, CR Park has a few landmarks that are familiar to the residents and worth seeing for visitors. In this chapter, we look at some of the important landmarks in CR Park.

## 2.1 Location of CR Park in New Delhi

CR Park is located in South Delhi, being surrounded by Kalkaji to the south, Greater Kailash to the north and west, Govindpuri to the east and Jahapanah city forest to the west. It is mainly a residential colony but has plenty of shops, dispensaries, bank ATMs and other amenities. It is located less than a 20-minute drive from Nehru place and Saket Mall.

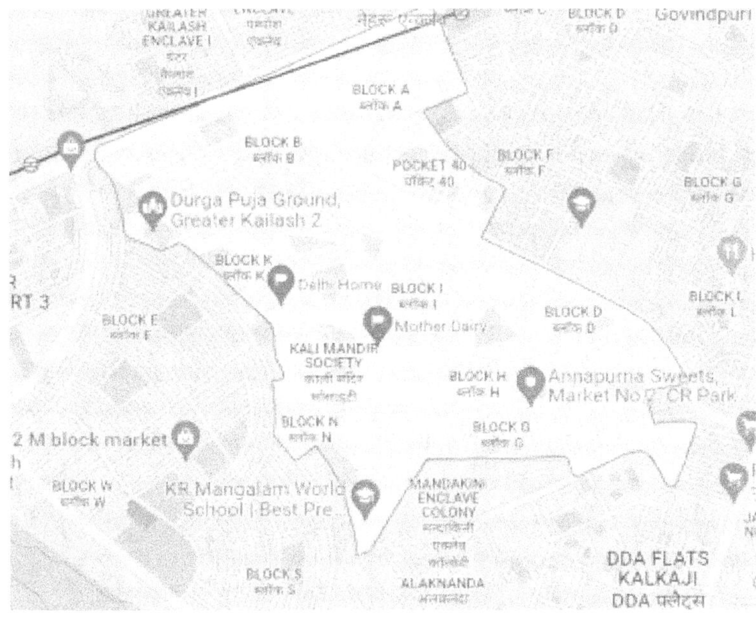


Figure: Map of CR Park showing some of the blocks, taken from Google maps

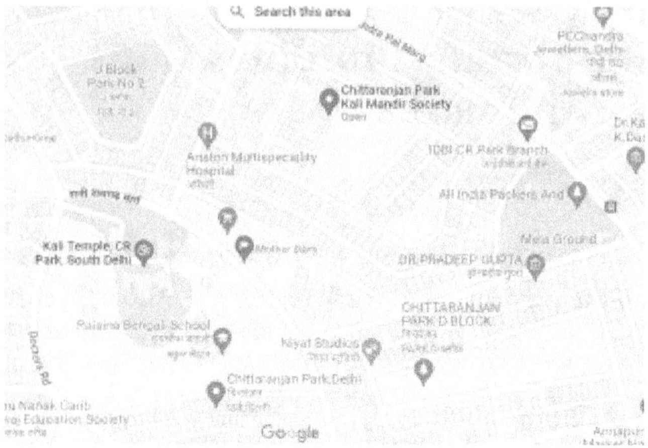

Figure: Area around the CR Park Kali temple, also taken from Google maps.

## 2.2 Residential Blocks

There are a number of Blocks in CR Park that are named in alphabetical order from Block A to Block K, with additional extensions called pocket 40 and pocket 52 added later.

Most of the residential blocks are now gated, with security guards at the gates to keep track of who is entering and leaving. Each block is managed by their own RWA or Residents Welfare Association, which are cooperative societies.

## 2.3 Main Road

The main road in CR park is called Bipin Chandra Pal Marg, which connects market 1 to market 2 and all the blocks of CR Park lie on either side of this road.

The lanes in front of the houses in the different blocks are narrower and often cars are parked on them.

Figure: Raisina Bengali School in CR Park

## 2.4 School

There is a school called Raisina Bengali School on the main road, established in 1970s, is English medium and follows the CBSE syllabus for classes from 1 to 12. It has Bengali language as a compulsory subject up to class 8. It has two branches, with one branch shifting to Mandir Marg, near Baird Lane in Gol Market and one branch remaining in CR Park. In CR Park there is a primary school campus in the main road and a secondary school campus near the Kali temple.

The address is: Raisina Bengali School, M & P-2151-52, Chittaranjan Park, New Delhi, Delhi 110019

There are also a few other schools and the campus of Deshbandhu college of the University of Delhi in nearby Kalkaji.

## 2.5 Parks

Each of the blocks in CR Park is well-planned, with one or more parks for kids to play and residents to do morning walks and exercise. Many of the parks also have seating spaces, jogging tracks and kid's playgrounds. The biggest park is called Mela ground and is close to market number 2. There are also many smaller parks such as the Khudi Ram Bose Park near K Block and Netaji Subhash Chandra Bose park near G Block.

## 2.6 Markets

There are four main markets in CR Park. Market number 1 is close to the Block C, Market 2 close to blocks D and G, market 3 close to blocks A and B and market 4 close to block K.

These markets have a good variety of shops such as mobile phone shops, grocery shops, barber shops, internet café, DVD and music shops, mobile phone shops, photo studio, Banik Dashakarma Bhandar, book stalls and food and sweets stalls. Markets 1 and 2 also have fish markets for buying freshwater fish such as Rohu and Hilsa, a favorite of Bengalis.

## 2.7 Cultural Organizations

There are a few Bengali cultural institutions in CR Park. Chittaranjan Park Bangiya Samaj and Deshbandhu Chittaranjan memorial society are two important institutions. They have buildings which are the center of cultural activities. Both of these are located near market number 1.

There is an East Bengal Displaced Persons' Association which has a building near market number 4 and opposite the kali temple.

There is a social welfare organization for women called Purboshree Mahila Samiti located in K Block. It also has a hall that is used for cultural purposes.

The addresses are as follows:

Chittaranjan Park Bangiya Samaj: Bangiya Samaj Bhawan, C-405, Chittaranjan Park, New Delhi, Delhi 110019

Deshbandhu Chittaranjan memorial society: J-1838, Bipin Chandra Pal Marg, Near Allahabad Bank, Block J, Chittaranjan Park, New Delhi, Delhi 110019

East Bengal Displaced Persons Association: I-1597, Block I, Chittaranjan Park, New Delhi, Delhi 110019

Mahila Samiti Hall: K1989, Chittranjan Park Rd, Block K, EPDP Colony, Chittaranjan Park, New Delhi, Delhi 110019

## 2.8 Temples and other places of worship

There are also some Bengali Hindu temples in CR Park, especially the Kali mandir. They are described more in the following chapters.

There is also a big Sikh gurudwara nearby in Greater Kailash 1, Arya Samaj in Kalkaji and a number of other places of worship.

Address of the Kali mandir is as follows:

CR Park Kali Mandir: CR Park Main Road, Kali Mandir Society, Chittaranjan Park, K1/54, Doctors Rd, New Delhi, Delhi 110019

Figure: CR Park Post office next to market number 4

Figure: Dr Kalyan Banerjee's homeopathic clinic

Figure: Ariston multi-specialty hospital building

## 2.9 Civic amenities

CR Park has its own police station which is opposite the main kali temple and near market number 4. This police station plays a big role in enhancing the safety and security of the residents.

There is a post office located in market number 4 on first floor. There are also branches of a number of banks and ATMs.

There is a garbage recycling center that is near to Mela Ground and market number 2.

A few allopathic and homeopathic doctors are also resident in CR Park and run daily clinics. Notable among these is Dr Kalyan Banerjee who is a famous homeopath and has won many accolades. There is also a hospital called Ariston hospital and a few diagnostic testing labs are nearby as well.

Savitri Cinema hall is located in Greater Kailash 2, a short walking distance from CR Park.

## 2.10 Conclusion

These landmarks, temples, parks, schools, and cultural halls, not only serve practical needs but also form the identity of CR Park as a living cultural landscape. With this grounding, let us now ascend the sacred hill to visit the most iconic religious site in the colony: the CR Park Kali Mandir and other temples that continue to be at the spiritual heart of the community.

# Chapter 3: CR Park Kali Mandir and Other Temples

In this chapter we look at the Bengali temples of CR Park, especially the famous Kali temple.

## 3.1 Kali temple on the hill

Also called Shiv Mandir and Kali Mandir, the temple complex is on a hill. It is made of three main shrines, dedicated to Radha Krishna, Ma Kali and Shiva respectively. The architecture of the three shrines is in traditional Bengali style and the walls have images of the Gods, also in Bengali traditional style.

Figure: The three temple buildings dedicated to Lord Shiva, Radha Krishna and Goddess Kali

Figure: Main Kali temple building, with traditional Bengali architecture

Figure: Inside of the main Ma Kali temple

Figure: Photo of the inside of the Ma Kali temple

Figure: Steps for entrance to Kali Mandir on the hill

The Kali temple celebrates most Bengali pujas such as Durga Puja, kali puja and saraswati puja. The prasadam and bhog is offered to the goddess and then distributed among the people. Often during the festivals there are long queues in the temple to collect the tasty vegetarian bhog.

The priests of the temple are also available to conduct Bengali Hindu rituals and ceremonies such as marriages, deeksha and shraddha.

The temple also arranges a number of Bengali cultural programs such as Rabindranath's birthday. For the cultural programs, famous artistes are sometimes brought over all the way from Kolkata and other parts of India.

The Kali temple also has a small library which has a selection of children's books, English novels and newspapers. It also runs a medical dispensary.

Figure: Sri Sri Balananda Dharamsala next to Kali Temple

The temple also runs a small Dharamasala called Sri Sri Balananda Dharamsala, where people from outside can stay for a short while, although it is advisable to book in advance. It also has a small attached vegetarian restaurant.

## 3.2 Kali temple in market number 1

There is a smaller but quite busy Kali temple in market number 1, right next to the fish market.

It has shrines to a number of Hindu gods especially Ma Kali, Shri Krishna, Shri Ram and Hanuman. It also celebrates important festivals like Durga Puja and Kali puja. On the days of the Durga Puja or Kali puja, one can give the pushpanjali at this temple and avoid the crowds in the bigger pandals. It also has arati of Goddess Kali in the evenings.

Figure: Visitors at the busy Kali temple in Market 1

Figure. Kali temple in Market number 1

Figure: Shani temple behind market number 2

## 3.3 Shani temple in market number 2

There is also a little temple dedicated to Shani Dev, just behind market number 2. The Shani puja is especially popular on Saturday evenings.

There is also a smaller temple complex in pocket 40 Navapalli in CR Park.

## 3.4 Conclusion

The temples of CR Park, especially the Kali Mandir complex, stand as powerful symbols of spiritual continuity and cultural resilience. They are not just places of worship, but venues of social gathering and celebration. With this in mind, we now turn our attention to the grand festivals that animate these sacred spaces, starting with the most iconic of all: Durga Puja.

# Chapter 4: Durga Puja and other Bengali Festivals

In this chapter, we discuss a few of the major Bengali Hindu festivals celebrated at CR Park. These festivals are the highlight of CR Park, having a huge crowd of people from all over Delhi coming to view them.

Figure: Durga pujas in CR Park, in a poster by Delhi Police

## 4.1 Durga Puja

Being the main Bengali festival, Durga puja is celebrated in a grand scale in CR Park. Almost every block has its own durga puja pandal, which is located in the park that is dedicated for each block. The whole puja is conducted usually in October as per the Bengali calendar. The public celebration is from Sashti to Dashami during Navaratri, along with daily rituals such as pushpanjali, arati etc.

Durga Puja is a huge cultural event for Bengalis, with lots of performers and children's competitions. It is held at the time of Dusshera festival and Navaratri.

The tasty bhog is a highlight of the Durga puja, with long queues in all the pandals near the afternoon time.

A typical Durga puja routine includes giving Pushpanjali (a flower offering) to Goddess Durga and chanting the mantras on an empty stomach, having charana amrita and prasadam, then having bhog in the afternoon, then witness the anjali of the goddess with beat of drums in the evening, along with cultural programs and shopping and pandal hopping with friends in the night. For Bengalis, one is allowed to eat non-veg food during the puja, and the dishes like mutton biryani, ghughni, luchi chola, fish chop and of course Bengali sweets are huge favorites.

During the puja, the whole area becomes overcrowded with Bengalis and non-Bengalis from all parts of Delhi seeking to have a glimpse of the puja. There are all kinds of food stalls erected at the pandals, as well as a fun fair for the kids.

The sites in CR Park and nearby where Durga puja is usually celebrated include the following (there could be more sites):

- B Block
- Cooperative Ground
- Mela Ground
- D Block
- E Block
- Navapalli
- Pocket 40
- Pocket 52
- Greater Kailash Part 2
- Kalkaji

The pandals are creatively and beautifully decorated. Many of these have won multiple awards for their innovative pandal designs in the past, featuring different themes such as environment, heritage, history, culture and so on.

Due to the burden of managing huge crowds and to prioritize the residents of each block in CR Park and also to finance the huge costs of the puja pandals, many of the Durga Puja organizers have a pass system for those who make donations to the puja. A pass allows two people to skip the queues when entering the puja pandal and thus save a lot of time. There is also a bhog pass which enables the holders to get the delicious vegetarian bhog of the goddess during lunch in the Puja festival days.

On the 10th day or Vijaya dashami day of Durga Puja, after the rituals are done, the organizers perform the Visarjan or the immersion of the idol in the river Yamuna. The usual site of Visarjan is in Kalindi Kunj site near Okhla, as designated by the Delhi government. Since 2019, the Visarjan policy has shifted to smaller sites including artificial tanks dug up and filled with water, so as not to pollute the Yamuna river too much.

During the Covid pandemic of 2020-2021 and the subsequent lockdowns, the temple was closed to most of the public and broadcast the daily arati and pujas via facebook live. They also had a facility for home delivery of bhog to residents at a nominal cost.

Figure: Durga puja being celebrated in the Kali Mandir temple

Figure: Beautifully decorated mela ground pandal for Durga Puja

Figure: A snapshot of cultural programs during Durga Puja in Navapalli Puja Pandal.

Figure: Shops in Mela Ground Durga Puja Pandal

## 4.2 Kali Puja

Kali Puja is an overnight puja to the Goddess Kali, on the same day as Diwali. Kali puja is also conducted in many of the same venues and parks as the Durga puja, but on a smaller scale than Durga Puja.

People keep a whole day fast for the kali puja. The actual puja begins around midnight and lasts for 2 to 4 hours. After the puja is complete, the devotees have the delicious vegetarian bhog offered to the goddess Kali.

Figure: Beautifully decorated Kali puja pandal at Market number 2

## 4.3 Saraswati Puja

Saraswati Puja is another of the traditional Bengali hindu festivals celebrated in CR Park, around the time of February and Vasant Panchami as per the Bengali calendar.

The festival is a favorite of students, since Saraswati is the Hindu goddess of learning and wisdom. It is usually held in the morning, and includes a pushpanjali of the goddess and chanting mantras on an empty stomach, led by a priest.

Figure: Saraswati Puja celebrated in a pandal in CR Park

Students and teachers from the Raisina Bengali school, a Bengali medium school in CR Park, take the lead in conducting the Sarasawati Puja. However, each block where the Durga Puja is celebrated also has a celebration of the Saraswati Puja.

## 4.4 Lakshmi Puja

Lakshmi Puja, dedicated the goddess Lakshmi who is the Hindu goddess of prosperity and wealth, is also celebrated in CR Park, usually a week after Durga Puja. It is usually held in the evening time.

Idols of goddess Lakshmi are put in the smaller pandals in each block park and worshipped. Many people prefer to do Lakshmi puja inside their own homes.

## 4.5 Cultural festivals

A few important Bengali cultural festivals such as Rabindranath birthday and Kazi Nazrul birthday are also commemorated in CR Park, usually with a cultural program including song, dance and plays. The venue for these is usually the CR Park Kali mandir, Bipin Chandra Pal Bhavan, Purboshree Mahila Samity and the auditorium at Bangiya Samaj.

## 4.6 Conclusion

The rhythm of life in CR Park moves through the beating heart of its festivals, with Durga Puja being the crescendo of cultural and spiritual expression. But even when the pandals are dismantled and the festival time is over, life in CR Park continues in its bustling markets. In the next chapter, we explore the vibrant local bazaars that provide the flavor, quite literally, of Bengali life in Delhi.

# Chapter 5: Markets in CR Park

In this chapter, we discuss the four market complexes in CR Park.

There are four markets in CR Park, numbered markets 1 to 4. The interesting this about these markets is that Bengali food, groceries and books are readily available, and almost all the shopkeepers, even the barber shops know at least a little bit of Bengali. Although many shop workers come from UP and Bihar, they have learnt to speak at least a few words in Bengali to cater to the mainly Bengali residents of CR Park.

## 5.1 Market number 1

Market 1 is a huge market with a wide variety of shops selling food, groceries and other items. It also has a Mother Dairy stall for milk items and ice cream, several street food stalls, CD DVD and mobile phone shops, Bengali sweet shops and a few Banik Dashakarma stores. It also has a barbershop and a photo studio. There is a fish market next to the shops. There is also a Kali temple. There is a flower shop nearby. Shambhu Book Stall has Bengali books and newspapers.

Figure: Shops in market number 1 in CR Park

Figure: Fish Market in market number 1 in CR Park

Figure: Durga Puja special "Sarodiya" books on sale in Market 1

Figure: Banik Dashakarma Bhandar shop in market number 1

## 5.2 Market number 2

Market 2 is possibly the biggest market in CR Park (or same as market 1). It too has a variety of shops as well as a fish market. It has a small shani temple behind the main market. It has a number of street food stalls and it gets crowded in the evenings.

Figure: Exterior view of market number 2 in CR Park

Figure: CR Park Market number 2 at night

Figure: Shops in market number 3 in CR Park

## 5.3 Market number 3

This market is located on a raised platform close to block A and B. It is a smaller market than markets 1 and 2. It too has a number of grocery stalls, flower shops and eateries. Tasty fish chops and fried fish cutlets are available in this market.

Figure: Shops in Market number 4 in CR Park

Figure: Barber shop in market number 4 in CR park

## 5.4 Market number 4

Market No. 4 is located next to the police station and in front of Kali Mandir. It has a post office, a barber shop, Mother Dairy shop, electronics shop, pharmacy, flower shop, food shop, sweet shop, Banik shop, grocery stores and bank ATMs.

## 5.5 Conclusion

The markets of CR Park are more than just commercial hubs; they are where memories are made, flavors are shared, and stories are exchanged. These spaces bring the community together in daily rituals. Beyond the shops and stalls, though, lie the parks and playgrounds that offer greenery, relaxation, and a space for leisure. We take a walk into these green parks in the next chapter.

# Chapter 6: Parks and Playgrounds

Every block in CR Park has an attached park and playground. They are named accordingly as well, such as B Block park, K block park etc.

These parks often have dedicated lanes around for people to do morning walks or jogging, a few slides and other items for a children's playground, benches for people to sit and relax and lots of greenery.

Sometimes, a single block in CR park may have multiple parks or playgrounds, depending on the number of houses. Each group of 10-15 houses is constructed around a small park.

## 6.1 Mela Ground

The biggest park is called Mela ground, where also the largest Durga Puja takes place.

Often the venue is used by youngsters for playing cricket and other games.

Other festivals such as Poush mela and cultural events also take place in Mela ground and the other parks.

Figure: Netaji Subhash Chandra Bose Park near market number 2

The presence of the parks makes the whole area much greener and pleasant and plays a role in healthier and pollution free air.

Many of these parks are used for playing cricket or football in the daytime by youngsters.

Figure: Children's playground in a park in pocket 40 CR Park

Figure: Khudi Ram Bose Park near K Block, behind Kali temple

## 6.2 Conclusion

The parks and playgrounds of CR Park offer much-needed breathing room and serve as informal gathering spots for all ages. From morning walkers to evening footballers, these green spaces are vital to the area's lifestyle. But what truly brings people together here, often even more than parks, is the irresistible aroma of Bengali street food. That is our destination in the next chapter.

# Chapter 7: Street Food in CR Park

There is a huge variety of Bengali style street food in CR Park.

## 7.1 Bengali street food varieties

A number of delicious dishes are available. There are phuchkas (also called pani puri), ghughni, momo, kathi rolls, fish chops, Bengali style mutton and chicken biryani and pulao and Bengali sweets such as Rasgulla and Chamcham.

Figure: Street food in market number 1

There are usually several food stalls in 1 to 4 markets. Most of them are for takeaway or parcel meals only, although some restaurants have chairs to sit on while eating. Many people nowadays use delivery apps such as Swiggy and Zomato to order from the shops.

Figure: People busy enjoying the food stalls in Market 1 during Durga Puja festival

Figure: Menus for street food in market 1

Figure: Bengali traditional sweets on sale in Annapurna Sweet house in Market number 2

## 7.2 Conclusion

Whether it's phuchka by the roadside or mutton ghughni during Durga Puja, CR Park's street food scene is as iconic as its festivals. But even amid food and festivity, there remains a love for the intellectual and the artistic. Let us now turn to the bookstores of CR Park, where Bengali literature and culture continue to thrive.

# Chapter 8: Bookshops in CR Park

There are a few bookstores in CR Park. There are also stationery shops in various markets. Shops selling CDs and DVDs of Bengali music and movies are also located in markets 1 to 4.

Figure: Ananda publishers' bookshop in Market number 2

## 8.1 Ananda Publishers Bookshop

Ananda publisher bookshop sells a variety of Bengali books including novels and plays and non-fiction by famous writers. It is located in Market number 2.

Figure: Shambhu Book Stall in Market 1

## 8.2 Shambhu Book stall

Shambhu book stall in market number 1 sells a number of newspapers, magazines and children's books, including Bengali newspapers Ananda Bazar Patrika and Bartaman.

Residents can also arrange to have the Bengali newspapers home delivered to their houses in CR Park from Shambhu book stall.

This stall is especially a good place to get the "Sharadiya" or Durga Puja special editions of Bengali magazines such as Desh, Anandamela and Nabakallol.

## 8.3 Conclusion

Bookshops in CR Park are small but mighty keepers of Bengali literary heritage. From Sharadiya magazines to timeless novels, these outlets feed the mind and soul. As we explore how Bengali culture thrives here, it's important to recognize the institutions that support and amplify these traditions. We now visit the cultural associations that form the backbone of this vibrant colony.

# Chapter 9: Bengali Cultural Associations

In this chapter we look at some important cultural and philanthropic organizations based in CR Park.

## 9.1 Deshbandhu Chittaranjan Memorial Society

CR Park is named after the great freedom fighter Deshbandhu Chittaranjan Das.

In his honor, there is a community building called Chittaranjan Bhavan and library just next to Market number 1. These are managed by the Deshbandhu Chittaranjan Memorial Society.

Many social activities such as medical testing, Bengali language classes, classes for kids such as karate and dancing and a library are arranged by the society in the premises of Chittaranjan Bhavan.

The website of the society is https://chittaranjanbhawan.com/ The address is C-405A, Chittaranjan Bhavan, Bipin Chandra Pal Marg, Chittaranjan Park Delhi, India 110019

Figure: Deshbandhu memorial society at Chittaranjan Bhavan

Figure: Library of Deshbandhu Chittaranjan Memorial Society near Market number 1

Figure: Chittaranjan Bhavan Bangiya Samaj

## 9.2 Chitttaranjan Park Bangiya Samaj

Chittaranjan Park Bangiya Samaj is an organization that promotes socio cultural events. It was set up in 1970. They have a big hall just next to Chittaranjan memorial society. The hall has a library, gym and auditorium where plays are conducted.

The hall can be booked by residents for conducting marriages and other cultural events.

The website of Bangiya Samaj is https://bangiyasamaj.org/

The address is: Bangiya Samaj Bhawan, C-405, Chittaranjan Park, New Delhi, Delhi 110019

Figure: Building of the East Bengal displaced persons association.

## 9.3 East Bengal Displaced Persons Association

This association is for supporting the persons displaced from East Bengal. They also have a building opposite the kali temple and next to market number 4, which can be booked for cultural programs.

The address is East Bengal Displaced Persons Association, I-1597, Block I, Chittaranjan Park, New Delhi, Delhi 110019

Figure: Purboshree Mahila Samiti Hall

## 9.4 Purbosree Mahila Samiti

Purbosree Mahila Samiti is a voluntary organization for the welfare of women. It also has its own dedicated hall which can be rented for cultural events.

It is located in K Block opposite the cooperative ground.

The address is as follows: Purbosree Mahila Samiti, K1989, Chittaranjan Park Rd, Block K, EPDP Colony, Chittaranjan Park, New Delhi, Delhi 110019

## 9.5 Conclusion

From community halls to cultural festivals, these associations are where heritage is nurtured and passed on. They serve as guardians of memory and custodians of tradition. Yet, to reach these places, one must navigate the practical aspects of urban life. In the next chapter, we explore how people move through CR Park, by metro, e-rickshaw, and more.

# Chapter 10: Transport Options in CR Park

CR Park has few direct bus services and the buses are also not too frequent. However, many auto rickshaws and E rickshaws are available to for the residents to commute, in addition to taxis.

Many of the residents also have their own cars, although car parking is a persistent problem. The newer style flats have a dedicated space in the basement or ground floor for car parking.

## 10.1 DTC Bus routes

There are a few buses that go nearby, mostly through Kalkaji but they are not too frequent. More frequent buses to parts of Delhi are available from Nehru place which is a couple of km away.

DTC bus 445 (New Delhi Railway Station Gate 2 to Kalka Ji DDA Flats) goes through CR Park, going from New Delhi Railway Station to DDA flats in Kalkaji.

Other bus routes are 449 (Old Delhi Railway Station to Ambedkar Nagar Sector 5), 490 (Rajendra Nagar R-Block to Kalka Ji DDA Flats) and 724C (Uttam Nagar Terminal to Kalka Ji DDA Flats).

Figure: Exterior entrance of Greater Kailash Metro station

## 10.2 Metro stations near CR Park

There are two metro stations close to CR Park:

- The Greater Kailash metro station, on the Magenta Line of Delhi Metro, is just next to Savitri cinema and very close to B block in CR Park. The closest metro station to the heart of CR Park is Nehru Enclave metro station, also on the Magenta Line, which is approximately 1 km from Pocket 40 and the A and B blocks.
- Nehru Place metro station on the Violet Line is also accessible, about 1.3 km from CR Park.

Figure: Electric powered E-Rickshaw used in CR Park

## 10.3 Electricity powered E-Rickshaws

E rickshaws have been recently introduced by the Delhi government in several Delhi localities including CR Park. They are electric powered, environment friendly and can seat up to 8 people. They are also very economical, a trip anywhere within CR Park should not cost more than Rs 20 per person in 2022. They can be hailed from any of the places within CR Park.

However, the E-Rickshaws usually will not go outside the colony since their routes are fixed. To go outside, one needs to take an auto or any of the other options such as buses, Ola and Uber taxis etc.

## 10.4 Other transport options

Ola and Uber taxis and other private taxi companies can also be used to commute to and from CR Park.

## 10.5 Conclusion

Understanding CR Park's transport landscape helps us see how connected this vibrant colony is with the rest of Delhi. Whether you're a resident or a visitor, reaching here is half the experience. But once you're here, it's no surprise that even Bollywood found it worthy of screen time. Let us explore CR Park's appearances in popular cinema in the next chapter.

# Chapter 11: Bollywood Movies with CR Park

CR park is also the site of a couple of Bollywood movie shootings. In this chapter we discuss them.

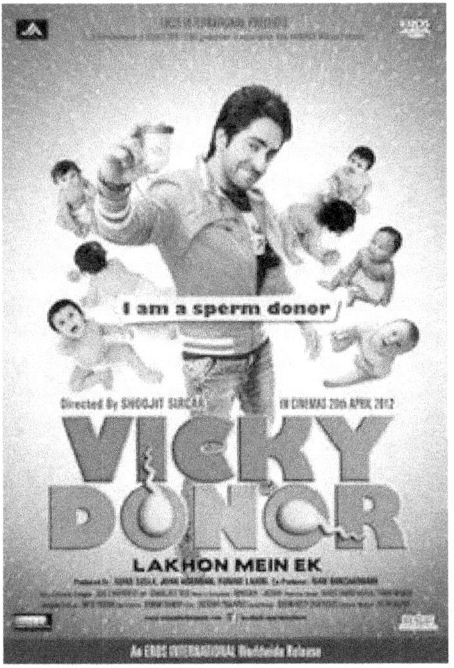


Figure: Poster for the film Vicky Donor (2012)

## 11.1 Vicky Donor

The 2012 film Vicky donor by director Shoojit Sirkar had some scenes shot in CR Park. The plot is about the hero who is also a sperm donor meeting a Bengali girl who resides in CR Park.

Figure: Poster for the film Piku (2015) based in CR Park

## 11.2 Piku

The 2015 film Piku, again directed by Shoojit Sirkar, starring Amitabh Bachchan as an elderly Bengali father Bhaskar Banerjee and Deepika Padukone as his architect daughter Piku had shootings in CR Park. It describes a long road trip by car all the way from their house in Delhi's CR Park to Kolkata at the insistence of the elderly father.

The interesting thing about the film in that it describes the life and mindset of a typical retiree in CR park living with his daughter, in a funny yet empathetic way.

## 11.3 Conclusion

The glimpses of CR Park in films like Piku and Vicky Donor showcase the colony's charm and cultural flavor to a national audience. But what these movies hint at, we now explore in depth - the wider spiritual geography of Delhi through its Bengali temples. Join us as we embark on a Bengali Temple Walk across the city.

# Chapter 12: Bengali Temple Circuit in Delhi (Beyond CR Park)

While CR Park is the spiritual heart of Bengali life in Delhi, there are several other historic and culturally significant Bengali temples across Delhi—especially in South and Central Delhi—that are worth visiting. Together, they form a Bengali Temple Walk, ideal for a weekend pilgrimage or cultural exploration.

This can be done as a half-day or full-day tour, starting from Old Delhi and ending in CR Park.

The Bengali Temple Walk offers a beautiful journey from Old Delhi to South Delhi. It weaves together temples, cultural landmarks, and stories of migration, tradition, and resilience.

Suggested Start: Early Morning

Total Duration: Full Day

Best Day: Sunday or any festival day

Transport: Metro + Auto/E-Rickshaw + Walk

Optional: Carry water, light snacks, and wear comfortable shoes

## 12.1 Tis Hazari Kali Bari

Start Time: 8:00 AM

Location: Tis Hazari, near Delhi Judicial Complex, Central Delhi

Nearest Metro Station: Tis Hazari (Red Line)

Tucked away in the bustling and institutional heart of Delhi, surrounded by courts, hospitals, and colonial-era government buildings, lies the modest but spiritually rich Tis Hazari Kali Bari. While not as well-known as the temples of

CR Park or Mandir Marg, it holds a quiet, dignified place in the hearts of many old-time Bengali families in Delhi.

The Tis Hazari Kali Bari is in fact the oldest Kali Bari in Delhi. The original idol was first established here in 1826, though the temple was destroyed during the 1857 revolt. The idol was salvaged and temporarily housed in Roshan Pura; the present temple at Tis Hazari was subsequently built in 1917. The temple is thus of great historical significance to Bengalis in Delhi. In the 20th century, the temple was further supported by Bengali residents of the area — many of whom were government servants, clerks, railway employees, and court staff. At that time, areas like Tis Hazari, Kashmere Gate, and Civil Lines formed the nucleus of Bengali life in Delhi, before the rise of CR Park.

*Time to spend:* 30-45 minutes

## 12.2 New Delhi Kali Bari (Mandir Marg)

*Close to Laxminarayan Temple, Connaught Place*

Nearest Metro Station: R.K. Ashram Marg or Shivaji Stadium

Arrive by: 9:30 AM

The New Delhi Kali Bari, located just a short walk from the iconic Birla Mandir, is one of the oldest and most prominent Bengali temples in the capital. Nestled along the tree-lined Mandir Marg, this serene temple has quietly served generations of Bengali families, tourists, and office-goers seeking a slice of spiritual Bengal in the heart of Delhi. Founded in the 1930s, shortly after the British shifted India's capital from Calcutta to New Delhi, this temple was envisioned as a spiritual and cultural hub for the growing Bengali population of bureaucrats, professionals, and clerical workers moving to Lutyens' Delhi.

It's beautiful, peaceful, and often hosts cultural programs. Great place for a quick spiritual recharge before brunch.

The premises also include a cultural hall used for plays, bhajans, and lectures, a small guest house where visiting sadhus or Bengali guests from out of town can stay, and a library and reading room with books in Bengali and English.

*Time to spend:* 30-45 minutes

## 12.3 Brunch Stop (Optional)

Try Bengali snacks at Bangla Sweet House (Gole Market) or Bengali Market near Mandi House if time permits.

## 12.4 Minto Road Kali Bari (Minto Bridge Railway Colony)

Location: Minto Road Colony, Barakhamba, near Barakhamba Road, Cannaught place.

Nearest Metro Station: Barakhamba Road or Rajiv Chowk

Arrive by: 11 am

The Minto Road Kali Bari is one of those quiet spiritual enclaves that often go unnoticed amidst the concrete bustle of central Delhi. This temple was established in the mid-1900s, primarily by Bengali employees of the Indian Railways who were housed in the nearby government quarters.

Located inside the Minto Bridge Railway Colony, this small but active temple is a beloved space for many Bengali railway employees, office workers, and long-time residents of the area. It is a simple temple with old roots, still active and cherished by the local Bengali community. Visit during puja times for a more vibrant experience.

*Time to spend:* 15-20 minutes

## 12.5 Ramakrishna Mission, RK Ashram Marg

Location: RamaKrishna Ashram Marg, Bharat Nagar, Paharganj, New Delhi – 110055

Nearest Metro Station: Ramakrishna Ashram Marg (Blue Line)

Arrive by: 12:30 pm

The Ramakrishna Mission in Delhi is not a temple in the usual sense—it is a living center of spiritual study, inner development, and social service. Founded in

1927, it was one of the early outposts of the Ramakrishna Movement in North India. For Bengalis in Delhi, it serves not only as a spiritual home but also as a cultural and intellectual haven rooted in the teachings of Sri Ramakrishna, Sarada Devi, and Swami Vivekananda.

It contains a tranquil main prayer hall with images of Sri Ramakrishna, Holy Mother Sarada Devi, and Swami Vivekananda. Aratis and bhajans are held daily in the mornings and evenings. Also has a vast library and reading room featuring spiritual classics, Vedanta philosophy, literature in Bengali, Hindi, English, and Sanskrit, a bookstore selling the complete works of Swami Vivekananda and other Ramakrishna-Vedanta literature, a guesthouse for monks, spiritual seekers, and visitors from across India.

*Time to spend:* 40-60 minutes

## 12.6 Dakshin Delhi Kali Bari (RK Puram)

Location: Near Sector-5, At the foot of Swamimalai hill, Opposite Swami Malai Temple Ramakrishna Puram, New Delhi – 110022

Nearest Metro Station: Munirka or RK Puram (Magenta Line)

**Arrive by:** 2:00 PM

This hidden gem is located at the base of the Swaminathan temple hillock. It's peaceful, lesser-known, and beautifully maintained. One of the few temples south of CR Park with active pujas and bhogs.

Founded in the late 1970s by Bengali families settled in RK Puram and adjoining government colonies, the temple was born from a desire to maintain Bengali religious traditions and create a spiritual community hub in an area dominated by Tamils, Punjabis, and other North Indian communities.

*Time to spend:* 30 minutes

## 12.7 Lunch Stop (Optional)

Have a proper Bengali lunch near CR Park or Greater Kailash – options include Oh! Calcutta, Bijoli Grill, or even homestyle food from a CR Park bhog line.

## 12.8 CR Park Kali Mandir Complex

Location: K Block, Chittaranjan Park, New Delhi – 110019

Nearest Metro Station: Nehru Enclave (Magenta Line, ~1 km) or Greater Kailash (Magenta Line) or Nehru Place (Violet Line)

**Arrive by:** 4:00 PM

The CR Park Kali Mandir is not just a temple—it's a living, breathing heart of Bengali culture in Delhi. Nestled atop a small rocky hill in K Block, this serene complex is a spiritual magnet for thousands of Bengali families in the city, and especially the residents of Chittaranjan Park, often fondly called Little Kolkata.

Founded in 1973 by the original Bengali settlers of CR Park—refugees from East Bengal and others from old Delhi—it has since grown into a sprawling complex of shrines, gardens, community halls, a dharamshala, and even a dispensary. The temple is both a sacred space and a cultural beacon. The campus also features a children's park and a musical fountain, making it a place of recreation as well as worship.

The main shrine is dedicated to Ma Kali, the fierce and compassionate mother goddess, worshipped with deep reverence in Bengal. Two additional shrines are devoted to Lord Shiva and Radha-Krishna, built in distinct Bengali temple architecture—with sloping roofs, carved walls, and terracotta motifs.

*Time to spend:* 1 hour

## 12.9 Market 1 Kali Mandir + Street Food

*Market No. 1, CR Park*

Close your journey with a short walk to this busy but lively temple next to the fish market. Then reward yourself with phuchka, ghughni, or fish fry from the nearby stalls.

*Time to spend:* 30 minutes

## 12.10 Optional

Visit Shani Mandir behind Market 2, or attend a cultural program at Bangiya Samaj, if your legs and heart are still game.

## 12.11 Conclusion

From Kashmere Gate to RK Puram, this temple trail uncovers a map of faith, migration, and community across Delhi. But even after a full-day temple walk, nothing compares to the electric energy of Durga Puja in CR Park. In the next chapter, we walk you through a day-long experience of this grand festival, from sunrise rituals to midnight feasts.

# Chapter 13: A Full-Day Durga Puja Stroll in CR Park

For anyone wanting to soak in the festive essence of Durga Puja in CR Park, a leisurely full-day stroll through its vibrant pandals, food stalls, and cultural programs is the perfect immersion. In this chapter, we suggest a sample itinerary to help you make the most of the experience - from serene morning rituals to lively cultural nights.

## 13.1 Morning – Start with Pushpanjali and Puja Rituals

Time: 8:00 AM – 11:00 AM

Where: Start at the Kali Mandir Complex or your local block puja (e.g., B Block or Mela Ground)

Begin your day with a peaceful Pushpanjali (flower offering) to Goddess Durga. The air is filled with mantras and the rhythmic beat of the dhaak (drums). Most attendees are dressed in traditional attire, white saris with red borders, crisp kurtas, or elegant Punjabi dresses. It's a spiritual start to your day.

Tip: Go on an empty stomach if you want to take part in the ritual.

Optional: Visit multiple pandals early in the day while the crowds are light.

## 13.2 Afternoon – Bhog and Bengali Flavors

Time: 12:30 PM – 2:30 PM

Where: Most major pandals (especially Mela Ground, B Block, Navapalli)

Once the morning rituals are done, follow the delicious aroma of khichuri, labra (mixed veg), beguni (fried brinjal), chutney and payesh (rice pudding) to the Bhog queue. The bhog is vegetarian, offered as prasadam to the goddess, and is often served on sal leaves or paper plates.

Pro tip: If you want to avoid long queues, get a Bhog Pass in advance by donating to the Puja committee.

Alternate option: If you miss the Bhog, enjoy a plate of phuchka or fish chop from the street food stalls at Market 1 or 2.

## 13.3 Late Afternoon – Pandal Hopping & Puja Shopping

Time: 3:00 PM – 5:30 PM

Where: B Block, D Block, Pocket 40, Cooperative Ground

After lunch, go on a relaxing walk through CR Park, hopping from one beautifully decorated pandal to another. Each pandal features unique artistic themes—environmental, mythological, or even global designs.

Take a detour to the stalls near Mela Ground or Market 1 to shop for sarees, jewelry, handicrafts, or books, especially the Durga puja special editions of Bengali magazines such as Anondomela and Nabakallol. Kids often enjoy the toy and game stalls set up temporarily for the festival.

## 13.4 Evening – Arati & Cultural Performances

Time: 6:00 PM – 10:00 PM

Where: Kali Mandir, Mela Ground Stage, Bangiya Samaj Auditorium

Return to the pandals in the evening for the Sandhya Arati, when the goddess is worshipped with lights, conch shells, and dhaak beats. It's a mesmerizing sight, especially if you catch it at the Kali Mandir.

Post-arati, take a seat at the cultural stage. Many local and guest artists perform Rabindra Sangeet, classical dances, plays, or modern Bengali songs. Children's dance performances and humorous Bengali skits add a lively charm.

Don't miss: Special guest performances, sometimes featuring artists flown in from Kolkata.

Evening snacks: Grab a plate of mutton ghughni, kathi roll, or mishti doi from the nearby food stalls.

## 13.5 Night – Last Pandal and Goodnight

Time: 10:00 PM onwards

Where: Your favorite pandal or the peaceful CR Park streets.

Wrap up your day with a quiet walk back through the softly lit pandals, now glowing under fairy lights and lanterns. Say a final goodbye to Ma Durga with folded hands, until tomorrow.

## 13.6 Tips for the Best Experience

Wear comfortable shoes or chappals – you'll be walking a lot.

Stay hydrated – especially during warm October days.

Carry some cash – many food stalls and donations still prefer it.

Respect the rituals – be mindful during anjali or arati times.

## 13.7 Conclusion

A day spent celebrating Durga Puja in CR Park leaves you with a sense of belonging. This is what CR Park offers not just during festivals, but every day. In our final chapter, we reflect on the essence of this unique neighbourhood and what makes it a cultural gem in the capital.

# Chapter 14: Conclusion

In this book, we have briefly discussed the main markets and other landmarks in Chittaranjan park or CR Park.

CR Park is important because it is a cultural gem, which preserves and promotes the Bengali culture in the middle of the national capital of Delhi. This enables the culture to be enjoyed by one and all. Anyone can visit and sample the tasty Bengali food and sweets, attend the Durga Puja festivities and listen to the Rabindra sangeet.

As all cultures, Bengali culture is also dynamic and changing, and a fusion of multiple influences. CR Park is a place where one can appreciate the richness of the culture.

It is hoped that this small guide may be useful to people who are visiting the area.

# Glossary of Key Terms

Adda — A cherished Bengali tradition of leisurely, informal conversation among friends, typically held at market corners, tea stalls or parks. A hallmark of Bengali cultural and intellectual life.

Arati (also Aarti) — A Hindu ritual of worship in which light (typically from a flame or lamp) is offered to a deity, accompanied by the blowing of conch shells and beating of drums.

Bhadralok — Literally "gentleman" in Bengali; refers to the educated, genteel class of Bengali society known for their love of learning, arts and culture.

Bhog — Vegetarian food offered to the deity during a puja and then distributed to devotees as prasadam. At Durga Puja, the bhog typically includes khichuri, labra, beguni, chutney and payesh.

Dhaak — A large barrel-shaped drum played during Durga Puja and other Bengali festivals. The rhythmic beat of the dhaak is one of the most evocative sounds of the festive season.

Durga Puja — The most important Bengali Hindu festival, celebrating the goddess Durga's victory over the demon Mahishasura. Celebrated over five days from Shashti to Vijaya Dashami, typically in October.

EPDP / EBDP — East Pakistan Displaced Persons / East Bengal Displaced Persons. The original name for the association and colony that later became Chittaranjan Park, established to house refugees of the 1947 Partition from East Bengal.

Kali Bari — Literally "House of Kali." A temple dedicated primarily to the goddess Kali, common in Bengali communities across India.

Mishti Doi — Sweetened yoghurt, a classic Bengali dessert made by fermenting milk with sugar, often served in an earthen pot.

Pandal — A temporary ceremonial structure erected for religious festivals such as Durga Puja, typically decorated elaborately with a theme. In CR Park, pandals are built in the parks of each block.

Prasadam — Sacred food that has been offered to a deity and is then distributed to devotees as a divine blessing.

Phuchka (also Puchka or Pani Puri) — A popular Bengali street food consisting of hollow crispy spheres filled with spiced mashed potato and tangy tamarind water. The Bengali version is typically spicier and uses a different water mixture than the North Indian pani puri.

Pushpanjali — A ritual flower offering to the deity, typically performed on an empty stomach, accompanied by the chanting of Sanskrit mantras led by a priest.

Rabindra Sangeet — Songs composed by Rabindranath Tagore, the Nobel Laureate poet and polymath of Bengal. These songs form a central part of Bengali musical and cultural life and are frequently performed at cultural events in CR Park.

RWA — Residents' Welfare Association. An elected cooperative body managing the affairs of a residential block, including security, maintenance and community events.

Sharadiya (also Sarodiya) — Special Durga Puja edition of Bengali literary magazines such as Desh, Anandamela and Nabakallol, published annually and eagerly awaited by Bengali readers. These editions are typically thick volumes containing short stories, serialised novels, and art.

Sindur Khela — A joyful ritual on Vijaya Dashami (the last day of Durga Puja) in which married women apply vermilion to the feet of Goddess Durga and then to each other, bidding farewell to the goddess until the following year.

Visarjan — The ritual immersion of the deity's idol in water at the conclusion of a festival. At Durga Puja, visarjan is performed on Vijaya Dashami, traditionally in the river Yamuna, though in recent years the Delhi government has designated artificial tanks to reduce river pollution.

# Other Books by Siva Prasad Bose

Introduction to Wills and Probate

Senior Citizens Abuse in India: And what to do about it

Introduction to Negotiable Instruments: As per Indian laws

Introduction to Marriage Laws in India

Neighbor Problems in India: And What To Do About Them

Managing Court Cases with Mental Strength

Self-Publish Books and E-Books in India

Delays in Court Cases in India

Introduction to Patents and Patent Law in India

Introduction to Property Law in India

Introduction to Tort Law in India

Did you love *A Walk in Chittaranjan Park*? Then you should read *Self Publish Books and e-Books in India*[1] by Siva Prasad Bose and Joy Bose!

[2]

**The Complete Self-Publishing Roadmap for Indian Authors**

Most self-publishing guides are written for Western markets. This one is written for *you*.

*Self-Publish Books and E-Books in India* walks you through every stage of the publishing process — from planning and writing your manuscript to formatting, cover design, publishing across multiple platforms, audiobook production, and marketing — with specific guidance for challenges that Indian authors face, including regional language support, ISBNs, and India-friendly platforms.

**What makes this guide different:**

**Platform-specific guidance** for Amazon KDP, Draft2Digital (now merged with Smashwords), Notion Press, Pothi, IngramSpark, and The Pencil App**Indian language publishing** — which platforms support which languages, and what to do when they don't**Audiobook publishing for Indian authors** —

---

1. https://books2read.com/u/mddD6E

2. https://books2read.com/u/mddD6E

including how to work around ACX restrictions using Findaway Voices**Budget-first approach** — free and low-cost tools at every stage, from Canva for covers to draw.io for diagrams**Modern marketing strategies** — from Amazon ads and Goodreads to BookTok, Instagram Reels, and email newsletters

Whether your book is in English or a regional language, fiction or non-fiction, this guide gives you the knowledge and confidence to publish independently — and professionally.

**Your readers are waiting. This book shows you how to reach them.**

# About the Author

Siva Prasad Bose is an electrical engineer by profession. He is currently retired after many years of service in Uttar Pradesh Power Corporation Limited. He received his engineering degree from Jadavpur University, Kolkata and has a law degree from Meerut University, Meerut. His interests lie in the fields of family law, civil law, law of contracts, and any areas of law related to power electricity related issues.

Read more at https://sivaprasadbose.wordpress.com/.